DROWNING SOUL

By
William Armstrong

Poetry in 5-7-5 and
5-7-5-7-7 beats

Evil compulsions
These are what you must conquer
You could rule us all

What's impossible?
Does it mean we shouldn't try?
That's the possible
The search for what is distant
Your success is in trying

Showing self-control
Doesn't mean you lack feelings
They just don't rule you

Such a tough summer
Most of it spent in the rain
Waiting for sunshine
Termites chew the house apart
Carpenters rebuild it well

When you are depressed
Lift those who are also low
Find your spirits raised

The parade sprints past
The rain leaves me cold and wet
Shivering warms me
An armed forces float glides by
Led by horses and banners

When sadness grips you
Don't dwell on happier times
That is not the way

A green-gold leaf drops
As it falls, my sadness grows
Harvest of autumn
Does winter hold any warmth?
Touch lit matches to tinder

The more that we learn
The more we doubt what we see
We seek more answers

A teacher has taught
I can now love the lessons
Where is the profit?
Bush strokes of nature paintings
Do not pay my food and rent

Keep hope always close
Thunder will follow lightening
Clear skies after rain

A song of struggle
Beats and notes sound readily
A cool, calming breeze
As in my youth on the pier
I cry for long, long ago

Don't disdain evil
The few souls it has captured
Suffer for us all

I'm torn rice paper
Words written on me falter
Few whole fibers left
I try to be papyrus
Lessons learned at denial

Actions define us
The weak give up the small ones
The strong persevere

A jaguar roars
He doesn't prowl; he watches
Old and weak; past it
Sleep is his calming balm now
Watch him and be comforted

Prove you're a true friend
Mix support with honest truth
Both will be believed

Two hummingbirds fight
Each hungers for the honey
Their long beaks questing
A whirlwind of wings and claws
A firestorm of longing

Passion's prisoner
The truth cannot move from it
Like us in quicksand

Dirt and leaves and rot
Sun shines between the shutters
Window frames broken
There is no front porch
Some snow on the roof

Kindness, compassion
If you would have all love you
Make these your habits

My cat adores me
Purring when I stroke her back
Begging for my food
She sometimes complains of me
And whispers of her hunger

Maintain composure
Do not be a spectacle
Shallow gets nothing

A reddish-brown rose
Full nurtured by Spanish soil
Weeds choke her bud
Her heady scent makes me reel
She knows he's not good enough

Keep what you say real
Not all want your opinion
Truth shouldn't be harsh

A stork starves and dies
Is the stork a metaphor?
Dried-up cabbage patch
Predict tomorrow a fog
Cold, lonely Zen example

Keep you tongue in check
Speak truth as if all listen
And not all agree

A warm, cool autumn
It's all about thanksgiving
Stir the calming breeze
A yellow, dusky morning
Sharpened turkey knife

Live in the middle
Avoid the harshness of poor
And problems of rich

Leaving Halloween behind
Goodbye to the horror show
Fall falls gently now
Shocks are blunted by coolness
Pain, stilled by understanding

Your words in action
Teach with few words, act with more
Show others the way

Know the source of pain
Worms devour coffee beans
Fireflies point the way
Bees sting my camellia bush
And I know of true beauty

Be friends with the bad
You'll find yourself hanging high
Above the abyss

Green, yellow, orange
Sweet Autumn warm dry coolness
Some dust-spattered leaves
Rich, full, tasty vegetables
I am mirrored and mined for meals

It is difficult
Repay rudeness with kindness
Be above the norm

Warm, lasting Autumn
Breezes, cool drinks of water
Summer's blast evolves
Crippled life becomes normal
A hummingbird heals my pain

Practice only good
Our time on Earth is finite
Know you have triumphed

Cinnamon, nutmeg, turkey
Store-bought pilgrims, paper leaves
Sweet potato pie
My fear of a carving knife
Giving thanks for love's dinner

Make your promises
Don't keep them, you lose your way
Keep them, you find it

A wind shivers me
Wonderful summer's goodbye
Autumn settling
Warm coats and long-sleeved knit shirts
Fallen trees regrown

Do not just promise
They are empty, without form
Keep obligations

The sun is still warm
Noon feels like evening falling
Nighttime is soul-black
There is comfort in the dark
A light vacuum for my pain

Don't be like a swamp
Muddy, unfirm and unwanted
Be like solid ground

All over the world
Seasons catch my hungry eyes
Nature's colors call
So, I reach out to find them
And smile in my futile search

They live, who are good
After death, their good lives on
Death is for the bad

A life of growing
Growing in long protein strings
Growing through nurture
Growth comes easily to Earth
Death must follow life and growth

Expect misfortune
When things are how you want them
You will be prepared

A golden-brown haze
It dims the cool, blue, silver sky
Alive and clogging
Shortening a too-short life
Wasting a too-brief moment

In prosperity
Be prepared for some hardship
Will soften the blow

A chatter-roar noise
A Doppler sound, come, then gone
Riding the city
Collecting helmet critters
Singing the freedom found

Enjoy your money
It is there to enhance us
But, be careful, too

Cool, blue unity
A wave of least resistance
All are swell flying
Lots of sand and seashell loot
Hearing and sensing the end

Prudence is the way
Money is great blessing
Don't make it a curse

Let the professionals
Watch talent and mind prevail
Meddle not with it
Your knowledge is scanty now
Don't watch your pride let you down

Calm your want for cash
There's more to life than money
It is just a tool

Wet misted vision
North storm flowing, drenching us
Rooftop waterfalls
Humid scented thunder pounds
Lightening flash crackle lessons

Work for you success
Lead in all your endeavors
But, remain calm, too

The snap of wet twigs
Leaf weight rain-heavy branches
Weak leaves cry and drop
Autumn water ought to fall
Grow the wet pile on the ground

Brag, you're something new
Tell us, no-one has seen this
You are much deceived

After-rain scented
Fresh smelling wet dusty dirt
Up-splash from water-down
Crystal reflecting tear drops
Precipitating heart-burst

The wise grow one way
By learning to live through loss
This is how we grow

Orpheus in hell
Strumming a lyre of healing
Classic strength alive
Classic tears to show us how
Playing notes to show us why

A garden needs care
Water it with heart and soul
To see it blossom

Called fall, cold Autumn
An end to muted colors
Stilled breezes silenced
Gentle, warm, moving colors
Just ahead, white, mounded snow

Be full with content
Learn what other creatures know
Contentment means full

Gone leaving season
Leaving leaves steeped, steaming heat
Tall fall going, gone
Love's shove showing below us
Tickle wick blown out

Look fear in the face
And then, your life will move on
And strength will be yours

See our 'us' growing
Trust our dust to solid ground
Loving governing laid bare
See all of 'me' in us all
Keep our cheap 'cheep' in silence

We are truly one
There is never 'them' and 'us'
We are unity

Golden fall folding
Silver-white winter opens
Red, yellow, green spring
Our life in myriad tastes
Your life is one-of-a-kind

What is our true foe?
Since all life is together
We are the culprit

Patience is plodding
Do nothing by halves or haste
Your efforts will fail
The slow-cooked meal tastes richest
Stir the pot and let simmer

Such thing as freedom?
No, it doesn't exist here
Chained to what is real

Your frame of mind rules
Poor does not mean unhappy
Sick does not mean death
Love the life you have, not want
You should decide what you need

What is real freedom?
Is it freedom from work?
To pursue our dreams?

Do you fight often?
Do you find yourself angry?
Do you want to yell?
'cause you are dissatisfied
Not with others, but yourself

True freedom can come
Once we learn to cope with life
And its ups and downs

Do they laugh too much?
Do they find humor always?
Even in the sad?
There are two reasons for this
They hide anger or sadness

Pain need not chain us
Once we learn to blunt its edge
And to stand and move

Worry is a lie
Anxious is an illusion
Your stress is useless
Believe it when you see it
Then, take care of the issue

Freedom from our pain?
Always find a doctor's help
Never fight alone

Oil is made by time
Gold is made by molten heat
Diamonds, by pressure
Tough times make a person grow
Life's bumps see us much tougher

Feel what you have to
And use it to move forward
Otherwise, you crack

Chill-wrapped autumn end
Afternoon still warm-cool breeze
Let's hope for more rain
Fashion-layered clothes-horse time
People seeing holidays

Build on the tiny
Learning step by learning step
To find your summit

Wisdom and virtue
Do they set our happiness?
Money, just so far
For, if the money goes,
What else to make us happy?

Do not hate your past
Keep yourself grounded in 'now'
Your past put you here

You should yourself
You must think of number one
Life is just for you
Think of yourself before all
Then, open your heart to all

Do not make it worse
Do a little, if you can
Bit by bit heals all

When you find yourself
That is only half the search
It has just begun
Now the real work has started
To find yourself in others

Trust to your instinct
If you find that you cannot
Then, trust in others'

Does something hurt you?
Is there something that damages?
Does something cause fear?
Then, recognize the damage
Do not do that to others

Do not self-pity
It is wasted energy
And you remain weak

Wrong choices mold us
A person of bad choices
Can find strength to change
But, a truly bad person
Can not be made to raise up

Sorry for yourself?
Sometimes, it's appropriate
Don't let it linger

The way of envy
When the mighty have fallen
And been too outshined
To speak as inferior
Those who have surpassed their place

Things seem bad for you
Things seem bad for everyone
Widen your world view

Middle-road riding
Extreme pleasure can soon fade
Temper the extreme
It is our human nature
Extremes are blunted by time

Appreciation
Our gratitude in action
Helps lighten our load

Sure, you find roadblocks
Every great effort has them
They're a part of life
They are what we need to win
Or none are impressed

Procrastination
How long do you plan to wait
To make your life great?

Strive towards every goal
See the dream in front of you
Work at it always
Don't value the end too much
The end might not satisfy

Why wait 'til later?
Life is happening right now
Get yourself moving

Prepare for bad times
Even if they don't happen
You should be wary
So, even in your good times
Be cushioned for disaster

Climb each rung higher
Step by weary step you move
Will you reach the top?

Action is the means
Don't be content just to know
You must also do
Do not just learn of a thing
Make what you learn part of life

Give yourself a goal
Have something that you achieve
That is your success

Harsh words are just that
Sounds and air said by the weak
Their truth is shallow
And as you grow and strengthen
Those words will sting less and less

Give critics the slip
Avoid their prying eyeballs
Don't give them your life

Surround yourself well
Take care with whom you are friends
They are part of you
As well as what you read from
Learn from words of hope and love

Anger has reasons
Argue in favor of rage
You will always lose

Take care not to brag
Don't boast of hoped-for success
Be sure of your plans
Wait until you have it all
You will be admired, not scorned

There's no real reason
Scream if you have to holler
The echo will fade

Approaching winter
Freezing heart-fires chilled stilling
Fanning fires ice-calmed
Death-blizzard in harmless bits
Ice crunching afterward strides

Is your anger just?
It probably is selfish
Live by example

Snowflakes swirling lace
Tornado snow season puffs
Worry for safety
Stop to inhale the beauty
Newborn once-in-a-lifetime

Can you stand alone?
Can you state your point alone?
Can you last alone?

Fall song echo out
Dusky pumpkin orange fade
Cornfield harvested
Lift the blanket of warming
Stretch and light the fireplace match

Do what you cannot
Change what you think you cannot
Focus on yourself

Feeling comfort food
Nature's well-worn happy hearth
Handmade quilted bliss
Every food for every taste
The Earth holds us close to her

See the world as you
View all the world as yourself
The same kind of love

Autumn/winter fight
Fall warring with winter chill
Warming freezing ice
Ice cube chilling hot soup
An all-out, snow-laden douse

Admiration fades
The admired and admiring
Be disappointed

Who's insulting you?
Do you find the slanders true?
Then fix your problems
Amend your character flaws
Otherwise, pay it no mind

Laughter moves mountains
Humor can shift the burden
Smiles lift the dark clouds

Pleasure is easy
Pleasure is quickly found out
Pleasure can be bought
Satisfaction is the way
Strength, perseverance and love

Your intoxicant
Why not make it your new booze?
Get drunk on laughter

The ultimate choice
We may not have much freedom
But, we do have choice
Choice to be content or sad
We have freedom to choose these

You are your best friend
Treat your best friend with kindness
Love your best friend most

The sun now shines bright
The clouds split slowly apart
Rain turns to drizzle
I still can purr and meow
But fur hides my skin and bone

People do not fail
Possibilities can fail
People do not fail

If your life were filmed
Would anyone want to watch?
Is it an epic?
Life can be an adventure
Give you fans their money's worth

Once you get started
Make your success a habit
Keep the win going

Appreciated
That word is known to us all
We want to be thanked
But, do you return the 'thanks'
Show your appreciation

What we call madness
Is often a way to cope
With an insane world

Love's variation
Many are the forms of love
None of them show hurt
Violence is not the way
Causing tears is not the path

You are your best gift
And your best gift is just perfect
What gift is better?

The past can stop you
Look ahead to move you
Don't look behind you
Walking backward, you can fall
Walking forward, you progress

Gossamer heart strings
Strum them with a fine, light touch
A breeze can do it

Afraid of living?
Fear of success or failure?
Your fear is the pit
Make the attempt with your all
Give all of you and you will win

Get rid of happy
Happy leads to unhappy
Contentment is best

Live for the present
Be here now, to enjoy life
No past or future
Know that tomorrow will come
Tomorrow will be your 'now'

Keep your vision clear
Don't let suffering cloud it
See life past the pain

Enjoy 'eureka!'
Discovery is your way
Delight you've found 'it'
Nothing makes work so much fun
As finding what you've searched for

Don't make matters worse
Don't fight hatred with hatred
Accept and move on

Be more generous
Do not take without giving
This creates a void
Love will disappear for you
All that's left are excuses

Hatred can drain you
Do not waste your energy
Save it to grow with

The world is ready
You need to work for your dreams
This will take effort
Show you want to work for it
The world will be there for you

Hit the starting line
Ready yourself and then go
Cross the finish line

Review your mindset
If you choose to be happy,
Set your mind on it
You can be happy or not
You must make that choice yourself

Give the best of you
Don't demand it is returned
You'll see it come back

Picky is okay
We all have certain standards
Stick to your choices
There is no-one born perfect,
Only born perfect for you

Make a search for truth
Once you believe you've found it
You must keep searching

Look past the beauty
Of course, see the package first
It helps decide us
But, the real gift is inside
Does the outside match the in?

Things are rough for you
Life makes it tough to go on
Others have it worse

Actions are our 'me'
What we do is our function
They are who we are
Not our promises, our words
These in motion inform us

Do not wait to act
The moment has just passed by
Do not wait again

Communication
We live as social beings
We must speak of us
But, words don't replace actions
What we do is who we are

Know and set limits
Too much kills the appetite
Wanting means searching

Your friends are your self
Look at who you keep close by
They tell your story
We gravitate towards ourselves
We look for support from us

Kindness is the way
It blunts swords and stills anger
It's easy to give

Your birth does not tell
Who we call 'common' are not
Ask the 'common' why?
All are born of two parents
All need air to live

How do you see things?
As they are or seem to be
Fix your view of life

Why must the sun set?
Why must we need 'finish'?
Why can't it 'forever?
There are no ending, just change
It is nature's way, to change

Like all livings thing
Growth is the natural way
It's life in action

Earth's community
Global unity and love
Peace for humankind
We can be all of one mind
Love is possible for us

www.ingramcontent.com/pod-product-compliance
Lightning Source LLC
Chambersburg PA
CBHW071834020426
42331CB00007B/1725